TURNING THE TABLES

FORWARD

Justin K. Johnson

Turning the Tables Forward

Copyright © 2017 by Justin K. Johnson

actnowinstitution@gmail.com

Printed in the United States of America

First Printing, 2017

ISBN: 9781541288454

6 Guidelines to Establish Growth and Success. . .

Turning the Tables Forward

AUTHOR'S NOTE

This is a work of nonfiction.

The examples I share are based on

the challenges I encountered, and

are reconstructed to the

best of my knowledge.

Turning the Tables Forward

1

ORDER AND UNDERSTANDING

"Understanding who you are and what direction you are headed."

How great is your testimony? This is an important question to ask yourself while on your journey of success. I believe that the bigger the struggle, the bigger the blessing has to be. One thing that I am not a fan of is struggling. I hate the idea of not being able to control certain situations that I face daily in life. I wish there was a button to wash away all the struggles of living.

While some things are more challenging to deal with such as death, I believe that it is necessary to eliminate as much added pressure as possible. What if I would have stayed with certain companies or job opportunities, or what if I would have been wiser with my decisions? Would the outcome be any different?

The most important thing that you can do for your personal growth is have a sense of direction. For years, I have put blame of my many different situations on someone else. I always thought that my actions were a direct correlation to how I was raised and by whom I was raised. While this may reign true to some degree, the most important factor to include in this equation is the choices or decisions I made.

I have heard many people say "For every action there is a reaction, and for every reaction it is a direct response to your actions." This means your actions have a direct correlation to the decisions you make. The decisions you make determine your future, and depending whether it is right or wrong, it could have a huge impact on your life. This means that you must have a grip on who you are and a sense of direction in which you are headed because your choice to make the right decision follows this foundation.

In fact, many people have big dreams. Most people have ways of achieving those dreams–I say most because others do not know how to achieve their dreams or even know how to begin turning that dream into reality. Understanding who you are and what you are willing or not willing to do, allows you to press forward with achieving those dreams.

Have you ever met someone and thought to yourself that this person has it all figured out? That may be because they have experienced challenges, whether directly or indirectly, or it could be they are in tune with themselves. I have come in contact with many successful people and have wondered how they gained such self-confidence.

I believe the answer lies in knowing who you are. Knowing yourself requires more than setting goals and checking them off in your "fixing my life" journal. It starts with educating yourself on the history of your family and searching within yourself to study your learned or practiced behaviors.

The old saying, "You reap what you sow" speaks volume to this scenario. While we can control certain parts of our destiny, other parts are influenced by genetics. I do believe that a great deal of what I have faced over the years has been the consequences of my own decisions, but consequently, some outcomes are related to the seeds that my ancestors planted before my life began.

I started searching for the real me after I was involved in a dangerous relationship, which I knew was going to lead me down the wrong road. Something that was intentionally meant to be casual turned serious. Long story short, it became so bad between us that I questioned was this person really after the good or the bad in me. After I discovered that her intentions did not benefit me, I knew it was time for me to make a change. The first step began with me leaving the relationship.

After we finally separated, I started to do some self-evaluations to better understand myself. Although the relationship was unhealthy, I believed good could come forth. I began reflecting on the things that made me happy and started seeking other things that gave me joy. Even though it was difficult, I targeted the negative traits that I had during that relationship and sought out solutions that would lead to change. For example, why was I an angry individual, why did I have a keen lust for women, or why was I sometimes jealous or negative?

I discovered that most of those answers stemmed from my family history. I grew up with a mother and a stepfather. My mother told me many stories about her transition from childhood to adulthood. My stepfather, very loving, was a hard worker and provider for his family. Although I had positive influences, I grew up with a lot of mixed emotions.

The normal urges of a young boy ran intensely through my bones. My main pursuit in life was to go after what I believed in (whatever that might have been), and this I credit to my biological father. He was very assertive and truly believed in going after what he wanted: whether it was women, money, or vehicles. Growing up I had the same tendencies and every time my actions got out of control, my mother was always there to correct and to remind me of my upbringing – stay on the path of righteousness and focus on that old time religion. Being that she knew my father's character so well, my mother did her best to keep me from repeating his decisions. She knew that it could lead to a downward spiral, if not monitored.

Being such aspiring leaders, my mother and stepfather taught me work ethics and showed me that a man provides for his family. At a young age, I knew what it meant to hustle and to earn money. However, I also learned what it meant to have notoriety and power.

I will be the first to tell you that power leads to a lot of unforeseen trouble. For me, it was jealousy that led to being disrespectful and angry. As a child, I grew up fearless and very candid. Speaking my mind about things that I considered important was never an issue. Whether it was right or wrong, I never withdrew from a heated debate. After understanding the things that made me and the negative impact I was making, it was time to make some constructive adjustments.

I began to spend a lot of time analyzing myself to determine how to become better. First, I began asking myself simple questions: What do I like? What don't I like? Where do I find my solitude? Then, I worked towards watching the company that I kept. Instead of entertaining others, I focused on simply enjoying myself. Lastly, I would meditate and listen to my body and its needs. To relax, I would cook, clean, and rest. During these times, I was able to hear more clearly and find understanding and balance. These strategies gave me the opportunity to achieve my goals and to help others.

I believe that you can overcome your struggles if you have the proper steps to see yourself through to the end. In order to have a story to share, you have to endure some opposition. In the beginning, when I asked, "How great is your testimony?" it was a question that speaks directly to your struggle.

You are not the only one who wants a better life. Reality may make this a difficult truth to follow.

Nevertheless, my plea is for each individual to remain wise and persistent. If possible, avoid stressful situations because in due time, a challenge will arise that will require your response.

TAKE ACTION NOW

During this segment, I want you to focus on you. Build yourself a guideline to follow and use this formula throughout your journey. The journey ahead is tedious but can get better as long as you have direction.

List five things that you enjoy doing?

    1.

    2.

    3.

    4.

    5.

List five things that you are not willing to do, whether that is now or going forward?

    1.

    2.

3.

4.

5.

2

VISION AND OBJECTIVE

"What are your dreams and/or goals?"

Words are weighty and very powerful. Every day I give attention to what I say and how I say it. Even though it is challenging, I try to be optimistic in every situation, whether good or bad. As a parent, I fall in love with the passion and demeanor of my children. I am always amazed at how fearless and eager they are at following the desires in their hearts. Whether it is walking, using complete sentences, or even reading and writing, they give it a consistent effort.

As a child, I grew up wanting to be anything as long as I was successful. Whether it was a fireman, executive chef, or a Wall Street investor, if it drew my interest, I wanted to be it. I spent so much time dreaming that a yearning grew inside calling me to live above the norm. The only problem with this automaton is that your dreams are attached to emotions, and if you do not believe in yourself, it is not easy to get other people to believe in you.

Since I was always flip-flopping about the things I wanted to do, most people did not take me seriously. There is no worse feeling than knowing something and not having the right resources to apply what you know. It is like having the secret recipe to your family's signature dish but not having dishes to prepare the meal. This is how I felt as a child as I was sharing my dreams with others. No one was able to connect me with the right people to push those visions forward.

Then, I was introduced to passion and desire. As previously mentioned, I come from a family of doers and hard workers. I know what it means to get knocked down repeatedly and still have the courage to get back up. I applied this resiliency in pursuing my dreams and achieving my goals. Life has taught me that there are many detours, but you must acquire the mindset of a warrior and keep fighting for what you believe in. I am always preaching to my children that warriors do not make excuses; they adapt to change and get things done.

When I was in college and things became

difficult, I either gave up or looked for an easy way out. I started noticing that I was the only one — so it seemed — who was not doing his classwork. I was not having the full college experience nor was I applying myself or networking. I was allowing my past to cripple my future until I saw other students applying themselves. Their determination gave me all the confirmation I needed. They were focused on changing their realities and headed towards a more promising future opposed to me, who was wasting time – something I vowed not to do.

I recall being in middle school, and the gym teacher would never allow us to play the full class period. We were wasting our time talking with one another instead of listening to his instructions. I can still hear him humming his made up song, "Talking up your time." This teacher taught me that wasting time causes you to miss out on the fullness of life.

After my reality check, I began networking and inquiring from different people why they chose their profession. Most people gave me stories which reminded me of my mother, but others were just looking to establish income. During that time, I related more with establishing income because I was a struggling college student seeking the profession that paid the most money. I soon discovered that this was not the approach I needed to take.

As my job hunt grew, so did my resume and frustrations. I was bouncing from job to job, searching for that "perfect" fit. Many times I was rejected, and for whatever reason, the interviewer always thought it was best not to move forward with me. This taught me to embrace rejection and use it as leverage for my breakthrough. Like me, you will face challenges, but you must believe in yourself and know that you will make it.

As time progressed, I realized that my rejections were nothing more than an experience. I have learned to reflect on denials, see how I could have handled them differently, and apply that insight to my current opportunities. After all this time, I am now gaining an understanding of my visions and what strategies will lead me to achieving my dreams. My first mistake was thinking that I had to have all the answers at once. I feared falling face first and hearing my family and friends say "I told you so." Nonetheless, you have to remain encouraged and press forward.

Another one of my misconception was viewing my life through someone else's achievement. It was easy to look at the success of others and feel that my dreams were vanishing. I consistently reminded myself that I did not know what the person did to achieve their level of success. In all fairness, I had to believe that in due time I would see the same benefits as long as I continued on my current path.

As you are achieving your goals, remember to revisit them. The key is to continue to focus on creating new opportunities as often as possible. Setting new goals will challenge you to grow, and there is a refreshing new adventure every day as long as you are planning for growth which is the number one contributor to success.

TAKE ACTION NOW

This segment is about moving closer to your purpose. Your decision alone has provided you the opportunity to fill in the blank.

1. As of today, I will make an effort to work towards

    _____.

2. List three short term goals.

    a.

    b.

    c.

3. List three long term goals.

    a.

    b.

c.

4. Create a vision board for yourself. Feel it with your dreams or ideas no matter the size big or small.

3

PLANNING

"A vision without a plan is only a dream."

Planning has by far been the most difficult thing for me to do. It mainly has a lot to do with my drive and ambition for success. While planning requires a more calculated strategy, I prefer to get things done fast and efficiently, more so, as a free spirit. Nevertheless, you have to believe in the formula in order to get to your divine purpose.

I have heard people talk about the joy they have now that they are following their dreams. It truly makes me want to follow their every move to achieve mine. The only problem is we all are uniquely created and have different paths to take. Following your dream is challenging and discouraging, but you must believe in yourself, apply the wisdom acquired, and wait for the harvest from the seeds you planted.

The first step in planning is changing your way of thinking. A positive way of thinking allows you to stay committed to your dream when others won't understand. When you are faced with the struggles of life, there are many different things going through your mind all at once, controlling your thoughts gives you the balance you need to move forward.

With me, I had to acknowledge that I hated the way my life was financially. I refused to allow my family to suffer through the struggles that were ever so familiar throughout my childhood. I needed to change the way we lived, and it started with me thinking as a success, even if I did not have much. I had to transform my mind in order for my brain to begin producing useful information.

For instance, I remember going to an interview and the interviewer asked me some very basic questions: Do you want the job? Will you give it all you got? Why should I not be considered for his company (a trick question)? Then, he proceeded to give me more practical advice, "If you were stretching right now and I asked you to stretch a little bit harder, you would reach out another inch or more. Every day you have to consider the inches of effort you are not utilizing." After considering his analogy, I began to incorporate it into my life. Your mind should be ready to perform and produce at any given rate.

The next step in planning is managing your time. Proper use of time allows you to stay committed to your strategy. With the rapid changes of technology, it is quite easy to waste time on meaningless things. Understanding that time is your most valuable asset could place you in position to grow. Warren Buffet said it best, "Some people prefer to watch television with their spare time, I prefer to review financial statements." The sooner I learned that time was a gift, the sooner I realized I did not have an eternity to figure it out.

I had to use the time that was given and become the most efficient person I knew. As a husband and parent I learned to get creative. I adopted the strategy of loaning my time to my employer and in return I would be receiving a check. Furthermore, I embraced the idea that the company I worked for was operating on borrowed time so I could no longer allow myself to have free time, even when we were not busy. With this time, I had to use it for learning new skills or building up a network base. This would lead to me having resources to use as leverage.

The final step in planning is practicing to become better. The lessons of life never reveal itself in the beginning. It took several crash courses before I realized that perfection only comes after the work has already been done. No one wakes up perfect at any skill. It is only after you have given that craft enough attention before you become an expert of that skill.

For instance, take basketball, one of my favorite sports. When I first started playing, the concept seemed pretty easy. How difficult could it be to place a ball in a circular hole?

This is when I learned a thing or two about skillset. As I mentioned before, we are uniquely created and have gifts that work for our advantage. The key is unlocking that gift and allowing it to flourish so that it can open more doors. In some cases, that unique criterion can be more than one gift.

When I began playing, there were clearly other people who knew more and performed better on the court. I considered myself competitive, so I was not going to accept defeat. I began to study the moves of the people who were better than me and started to understand the importance of having "the touch." Growing up, Allen Iverson was my favorite basketball player. I considered him to be the greatest player of my time. His determination sent the message that he must be heavily guarded. To add to this, his talents and leadership spoke volume. I soon learned that Allen Iverson had "the touch."

My older brother also played a key part in my success by teaching me to use what I have. He taught me the purpose for the box on the back of the backboard. Tim Duncan, who was by far the greatest power forward on and off the court, had the sweetest kisser off the glass. I embarked to practice his moves and soon became pretty confident enough to go after my competition. I challenged them and it turned out to be worth my efforts. My strategic plan of learning from the sidelines paid off.

As of today, I still believe these simple strategies are important. Along this journey, I have gotten away from thinking that planning is a simple step-by-step concept and have embraced the fact that those who are successful look at planning in a more strategic manner.

I challenge you to allow your mind to dismantle new barriers of opportunity. Envision triangles in a room full of squares by not limiting yourself to only a box way of thinking. Although learning how to plan was accidentally discovered through my experiences, it provided me with a foundation to begin building my story of success.

TAKE ACTION NOW

In this segment, I want you to focus on creating your pathway. Keep in mind the formula: *the thought process, time management, and practice.* There are no short cuts to success, but a sense of direction can keep you grounded and focused on the adventure that is ahead.

**Note: In this section, it is best to start with your goal and focus on answering the remaining questions while on the journey.

1.   What is the first step in reaching your short/long term goal(s)?

2.   What resources are available for you?

3.   What defines (insert goal)?

4.   How does it become reality?

4

PATIENCE

"Nothing planted today bear harvest the same day."

I love the Animal Channel! It is something about seeing animals in its natural habitat that gives me a great appreciation for life. Growing up, we watched a lot of animal shows. I never questioned my parents as to why, I just watched for entertainment as I thought I should. Now that I am older, I reflect on the genius mindset of my parents. The mystery behind watching the animal shows allowed my mind to wander. This essentially led to the discovery of different animals, their habitat, and their ways of survival. Whenever I inquired about the different animals, my parents were always able to provide me with an answer. Whether if they were right or wrong is debatable, but the fact still remains that I was learning.

Some animals in particular that I admire are hawks, lions, and orcas. I believe these animals are the alpha predators, respectively. I love the poise and patience of these creatures. It just amazes me at how perfect they are at lurking on their prey. Of course, nothing starts off in ready form. Through their constant desire for food in order to survive, these animals had to adopt plenty of patience and suffer several crash courses. After trial and error, they were eventually able to perfect their skills.

The hawk by far has the best vantage point when it comes to identifying its prey. The hawk never swoops right away on its target but takes the time to study the subject's pattern. Then, at the right moment, it dives fiercely down as a soaring missile in attack mode apprehending its meal. Similar to the hawk, the lion spends hours watching its prey waiting for the best moment to attack. Most animals' response is too slow to counter or escape when this beast takes the prowl. As far as the orca, this is the most intelligent predator of them all. It spends its time tormenting its prey for sport by tossing it back and forth amongst its group or pod until it feels it is time to turn play into food. For the orca, its intelligence is a key component in its ability for hunt because it likes to wear down its prey before a feast.

The most important trait these genius animals have in common is patience, and this is where I have learned to craft my skills. The saying "patience is a virtue" left me baffled for a long time. I never knew the meaning, but now that I am older, I can say aged wine tastes better than freshly brewed wine any day. The young me spent a lot of time doing and doing without ever considering that some things take time to perfect.

Life has shown me that in this era of technology, we all want things readily made. Technology has allowed for the advancement and urgency of many things we enjoy every day now. In contrast, time has shown me, there is nothing new under the sun.

Looking back at history, I can reflect on the hunting and gathering era where the masses of people had to wait quite often to eat. More often than we are aware, hunters first had to learn what tools they could use for hunting. On many occasions, they were under prepared because of lack of proper artillery. After many encounters of practice, they were able to proceed forward. Furthermore, the community spent many hours a day and sometimes nights waiting for a kill. After the kill, the gatherer had to prepare the carcass for eating. Until the pattern was perfected, this was the routine of each respective territory.

I believe we spend a majority of our time focusing on expeditious solutions. One thing we have to consider, no matter how much we force things to happen, time has its own way of operating. As I like to say, "time is lazy" but in reality, I was just getting ahead of myself. I had to slow down and admire the small things along my journey. There is only one way to perfect your craft, and patience is the gatekeeper.

Something else I became mindful of was the idea of patience not always being equated to waiting. I learned that it also includes not forcing things into existence. To explain, I remember as a child when my mother and stepfather bought puzzles for my sister and me. While the main goal was to achieve a finished product, I had a difficult time making it past the outer frame of the puzzle. (Troubling, I am aware.) The pieces always looked as if they should fit wherever I wanted them to go. The problem was I could not force them into where they were not designed to go. I was trying to change the configuration of the puzzle, but by not forcing, I learned to appreciate the art of puzzles.

I have discovered that, while my passion may want me to do one thing, time has its way of providing me with educational lessons. These lessons have taught me the difference between what is factual and what is a myth. I also learned that when you force things into existence before season, it never turns out as intended. In response, I constantly reminded myself not to take on more than I can handle.

When an opportunity is presented, move forward and apply what you have gained. Not all information is for the present time. Learn to create a mental storage for the information that can be applied to your life at a later date.

Life shows us daily that dreams can be accomplished, but we must allow patience the opportunity to make us whole so that we can achieve more. It has shown me that though we want everything instantaneously, we should see things through to the end. I am even more motivated to reach my goals and become a more responsible husband and parent through this lesson. Because in the end we do not win, until we all are winning.

I believe that if you consider yourself a follower of this teaching, you are already on the right path. As you continue to battle the challenges of today, I want to encourage you to believe in the process and allow time to bear fruit for the things that are important.

TAKE ACTION NOW

In this world of technology, it is easy to get ahead of our situations. During this segment, I want you to focus on regaining your ability to wait.

Is there anything today that you can put off until a later time? Write down two things that are making your schedule "full."

1.

2.

Name a goal that has been on your heart. It can be spending time with family, working on a budget, etc.

Focus on including your goals into those open time slots that you now have available.

5

THE PROCESS

"Time is not as important as the process. No matter
how long it takes, fall in love with the journey."

"I will trust in the process. I will trust in the
process." This chant has fueled me over the years. Fear
of the unknown made me very uncomfortable in the
beginning of my journey. I consciously knew I was
making the right decision, but I needed something to
keep me going and there my chant was cheering me on
with encouragement. Starting my pursuit was as
difficult for me as being stranded in the middle of the
woods, waiting forever for assistance only to realize it
was never going to come. That is when I made the
decision to encourage myself and see my way through
to the end. In moments such as this, my natural
instinct chimed in to remind me that I was capable of
achieving anything with a calm spirit, and so will you.

Throughout my journey, life has shown me that
staying positive in any situation will keep me stable

and allow me to persevere in spite of any obstacle. I recall taking jobs that I was not completely satisfied with or working extra hours to provide for my family. I wanted to quit, but the wellbeing of my family was my top priority. Whenever I would wake up not knowing what was ahead, I would take a deep breath and say, "Trust in the process."

To understand what the process entails, you have to understand the importance of time. Time is a mystery because you never know what might occur within the next moment. One minute, you could be having the time of your life and on the opposite end; you could be facing a major tragedy. One thing is for certain regarding time; it is constant and consistent, so this allows you to prepare accordingly.

Life will hand you lemons, but time allows you to convert those lemons into lemonade through trial and error. Growing up I heard many people say that time waits for no man, or woman. I will go a step further and say that time will not change for anyone not even for your needs. I have learned with all things being constant that you get out of life what you put into it. If you put forward the effort in achieving something, in due time you will see the fruits of your labor. While waiting, I chose to give my time to those who would benefit from it the most, my family. I began setting goals for us and made the conscious decision to give my efforts to the things that I could control.

I grew up wanting my father's influence. Although my stepfather did all that he could do, nothing could replace the void of not being able to share important things with my biological father. Now that I am father, I know the importance of having a masculine role model. My job is to validate my children, assure them that it is acceptable to take risks and to try new adventures. Also, our ability to bond has shown me, that though I might not "have it all," the love and joy of each other's company surpasses any need that we may have. My children never look at me and think of me as nonexistent or not a role model. My parents taught me long ago that joy comes from within. Neither the world nor anyone can grant you this blessing.

My siblings and I did not grow up with much, but I felt that we did not lack anything. We ate and played every day and slept well at night. We were taught to appreciate what we had, and these are the values that I share with you today. Life brings many challenging circumstances, but going home and giving my heart to the people who love me has allowed me to remain focused. There are countless options for you take advantage of, such as self-worth, but for us, I wanted to change the exposure my family had.

To add to this, your support system will play a major role in your success. Not everyone will understand your vision, but you will need people in your corner that will stand out and stand up for you. If it were not for the love from my family, I would not be half of the man that I am today.

Staying committed to this process has served as the best teacher for me because now I understand the importance of waiting. I believe unfavorable situations are the pit stops we take in life as we are transitioning into success, however, as long as you remain on the course, the road ahead levels over. For instance, the responsibility of providing for my family took me away from home. Trying to earn extra income, I clocked a lot of overtime hours at work. Whenever I called to tell my wife that I would be late, I could tell that it was sucking the life out of our marriage. However, she never complained but actually stood firm in our love and supported me far more than I did myself at times. This allowed me to carry on with our goals and create opportunity for us that would impact our way of living.

During this phase, we chose to refocus and reprioritize our goals because someday we knew the tables would turn in our favor. Instead of discussing work in the evening, we discussed ways to fund our dreams. We, also, spent a vast majority of the little time we had building trust and communicating. Every decision we made we were sure to include the other person's input because our decisions were going to impact us as a whole. Neither of us wanted to be underprepared and we respected each other enough to include each other's perspective.

Life has taught me that how you handle circumstances will determine your exit. When things are going your way, it is easy to be enthusiastic and to become sidetracked. I am wise enough to know that there are many peaks and valleys along the road in life, in spite of that, during either time I knew to praise The Most High as often as I could.

You must acknowledge how you arrived at your current position because life has a way of humbling you. At any moment, the tide will turn and life will present its next hurdle. To stay focused, I reminded myself of my goals, examined my past complications, and concluded that there is always a test before every new chapter. Then, I showed appreciation to God for the growth that I had endured and pressed forward.

Growing up, I often heard "The more praise you give the more blessings you will receive." I believe, while God does hear our every prayer, there is nothing like showing gratitude for the things we already have. It reminds me of my mother's familiar aphorism, "Open your back door."

While life may have previously been challenging, your journey ahead has already been prepared. The simple thing to do is remember the process you adopted during the struggle and apply it in the present time. Life is full of new chapters and many doors, and the ones you make it through should be used as a pad to launch others forward.

TAKE ACTION NOW

During this chapter, I concentrated on showing you how to get the most of the precious gift of time. What do you plan to do right now, until time permits?

During this segment, do not give attention to your situation but focus on the things that may have gone unnoticed.

- Today is a good day to tell someone that you love them. Focus on a relationship that you have with someone that you have not been on great terms with. Give them a call; see them face to face, or whatever you need to do to resolve the issue.

- Remind someone how much you appreciate them. A small gesture goes a long way. Consider your loved one or a friend. Have they gone the extra mile for your sacrifice? Consider returning the favor.

- Explore an old hobby or create a new one. A lot of time we put our hobbies on the shelf, as if it were a trophy. Hobbies are what allow you to remain focused.

- Be kind to a stranger. Consider listening to someone. Sometimes people need to hear their thoughts aloud so that they can create a solution.

6

SHOWTIME

"This is the moment before; leave it all on the table."

Empowerment is vital. I discovered what motivates me is overcoming obstacles. I enjoy getting to the root of the problem and discovering a solution. Some people find motivation through music and others through daily routines or rituals. Whatever the choice, the key is to engage in daily conversations with yourself in order to stay focused on the task that may define your life.

Preparation is highly critical to achieving greatness. It will determine your success or failure. On opening night, if an actress is not prepared and does not remember any of her lines, her career will suffer or possibly end. However, life is about making the best of any situation. During trials and tribulations, you have to allow them to influence you to do better. Quite often we believe the circle of life is about repeating the past. In some instances, this could be accurate, on the contrary, it is more about overcoming setbacks and not wasting too much time and energy on circumstances you have already experienced. Instead, you should acknowledge the experience and press forward to better opportunities.

What has influenced me to keep pressing forward is revisiting my past and paying attention to the details. Being detailed is important because it is what set us apart from the next individual. If it were not for our differences, then we all would be qualified to do the same tasks. Regardless of my belief that I can do all things, I choose not to put forth the effort in everything that I am capable of doing. In most cases, I am willing to pay someone for their expertise. Professionals, such as doctors and mechanics, have dedicated their time and livelihood to perfecting their craft. In contrast, the skills I possess are due to the preparation and dedication I acquired to make me an expert in my respective career.

I remember going to the movies with my older siblings one day. I thought I was going just to enjoy the newest film that was trending for the summer, but in reality, it was a test to see how much of the details I was really paying attention to. I remember leaving out of the theater and being asked, "What was the purpose of the movie?" Here I was—no more than eight or nine—trying to analyze a film. Afterwards, I felt as if there was no purpose. As I have grown older, I have discovered that being observant and meditating on previous experiences is highly effective. There is no way to fully understand someone else's vantage point, but through these resources we are able to understand an individual's way of thinking.

Life has handed me many obstacles. Until I learned how to embrace the challenges, I didn't discover the advantage of leaving it all at the table. I can recall sitting in the car getting ready to go into the office of a potential employer. I would encourage myself by saying, "This is the moment you have dreamed of, show time." In the end, I was rejected. Whenever I was eligible to do something, there was always a "sorry not at the moment" conversation.

I teach my children how to adapt to any situation. While I may not have been able to get a particular job, there were always many other ways to adjust and get the best of every opportunity.

I grew up dreaming that every day I was on the national stage. Life was the cameraman, and I was the main character. Although I did not consider my life to be a script, I always envisioned getting to the end of the story and telling my children, and their children, that this was the story of my life. Show time!

I believe the only way to fully embrace life is to change the person whom is speaking. Until you become the narrator of your story, someone can always tell you "not at the moment." I believe every "no" I received was only a reminder for me to remain on the course of my journey in order to embrace the many "yes" opportunities I have and will continue to receive.

When I first began writing this book, I was a rock wedged in between several stones. All I needed was an indication to show me that I was making good decisions. That is when I came up with the idea for every chapter. Every chapter represents a challenging moment that I encountered along my journey. It required me to be the narrator of the outcome. Whenever I entered a new chapter, I would refer to my subtitles to give me the strategy on how to narrate the journey. This was my execution strategy.

Execution is the sum total of practice and assurance. For example, the Olympic Games are held every four years, but the timeframe does not downplay the importance of the event or the training of the athletes. These athletes spend years preparing for this moment because this represents their struggle, their country, and their loved ones. Most of them have dreamt of seizing this opportunity since their youth so through practice and assurance they know what preparations to take, such as what to eat and what activities to partake in. Like the Olympian athlete, I am able to execute because of the preparation and perseverance that I have already endured. Once I made the commitment to strive in my excellence, the joy and passion came without any effort.

Your commitment to achieving better has allowed you to make it this far. Continue to draw from your difficulties and allow them to push you to your goals. In order to appreciate the full journey, embrace your shortcomings instead of doubting yourself. If I had given up, I would have never discovered who I am.

Turning the Tables Forward

REFERENCE GUIDE

I have provided you with the steps and subtitles for each chapter. Consider displaying them on your goal boards to remind yourself what steps you need to take to get through your current phase. As I informed you in the text, these are the steps my family and I utilized to see us through our drawbacks.

I pray for blessings upon your life and accept your inadequacies …

1. **Order and Understanding**
   - Understanding where you are and where you are headed.

2. **Vision and Objective**
   - What are your dreams and/or goals?

3. **Planning**
   - A vision without a plan is only a dream.

4. **Patience**
   - Nothing planted today bear harvest the same day.

5. **The Process**
   - Time is not as important as the process. No matter how long it takes, fall in love with the process.

6. Showtime

- This is the moment before; leave it all on the table.

ABOUT THE AUTHOR

Justin K. Johnson is a management professional with eight years of experience in customer service, sales, and marketing. He has a proven track record of combined leadership, organization, delegation, and teamwork skills within a well-established management setting creating profitability and success.

Justin's areas of expertise include:

- Leadership
- Organization
- Counseling
- Forecasting/ planning
- Problem Solving
- Praise and recognition

- Team building
- Public speaking
- Multi-tasking
- Inventory Control
- Motivational speaking

- Negotiation
- Marketing
- Critical thinking
- Auditing
- Praise and recognition

To book Justin Johnson for your next conference or in-house event, please email:

Justin Johnson
actnowinstitution@gmail.com with the heading "Booking Info".

He regularly shares his experience and advice on most social media platforms:

www.writingmotivates.wordpress.com

Facebook Fan Page: Justin K. Johnson

Linkedin: Justin K. Johnson

Twitter: @nySjohnson

ACKNOWLEDGEMENTS

This has been a surreal experience that I am forever grateful to have been a part of. It is with deep gratitude that I would like to thank everyone that made this book a possibility. A special word of thanks goes to my wife, Aquila, who is the glue behind the scene that held this whole thing together. If it was not for her, this would all still be a dream in my mind. I love you and thank you for not giving up on me.

Also, a warm thank you goes out to Lady Walker and Maggie McGriggs for allowing me to use their platform. You both believed in the vision well before this moment, and I am grateful to have become acquainted with you.

To so many others who also contributed your thoughts and support, I share much gratitude for you. You are the true inspiration and I hope many blessings fill your life.

It has been a pleasure and look for more soon.

Justin K. Johnson

Turning the Tables Forward